The Less You
PREACH
The More You
LEARN

Also by Shashi Tharoor

NON-FICTION

Ambedkar: A Life
Pride, Prejudice, and Punditry: The Essential Shashi Tharoor
The Battle of Belonging: On Nationalism, Patriotism, and What It Means to Be Indian
Tharoorosaurus
The New World Disorder and the Indian Imperative (with Samir Saran)
The Hindu Way: An Introduction to Hinduism
The Paradoxical Prime Minister: Narendra Modi and His India
Why I Am a Hindu
An Era of Darkness: The British Empire in India
India Shastra: Reflections on the Nation in Our Time
India: The Future Is Now (ed.)
Pax Indica: India and the World of the 21st Century
Shadows Across the Playing Field: 60 Years of India-Pakistan Cricket (with Shahryar Khan)
India (with Ferrante Ferranti)
The Elephant, the Tiger, and the Cell Phone: Reflections on India in the 21st Century
Bookless in Baghdad
Nehru: The Invention of India
Kerala: God's Own Country (with M. F. Husain)
India: From Midnight to the Millennium and Beyond
Reasons of State

FICTION

Riot
The Five Dollar Smile and Other Stories
Show Business
The Great Indian Novel

For my grandchildren
Eliseo Kailash, Ximena Anahita, and Kahaani
in the hope that some of these thoughts
might strike a welcome chord one day.

–SHASHI THAROOR

For all those I could never do justice to.
And they are legion.

–JOSEPH ZACHARIAS

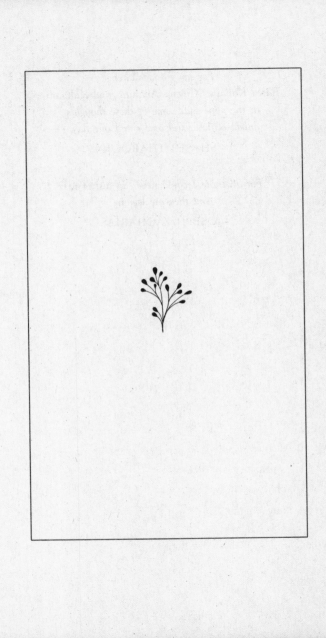

CONTENTS

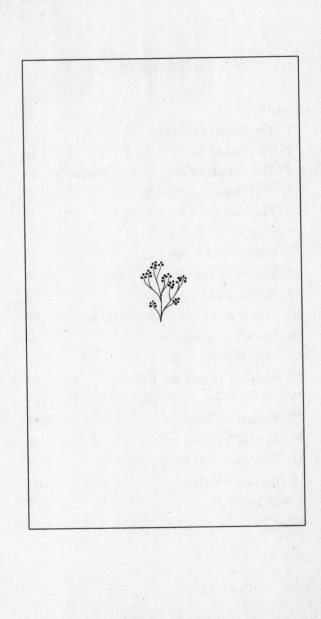

INTRODUCTION

I first met Joseph Zacharias when I set up an academy of business communication in Thiruvananthapuram shortly after leaving the United Nations in 2007. The academy was intended to respond to a perceived need for improving spoken English and comprehension skills amongst otherwise well-educated Malayalis whose mastery of English was often confined to the written word. In our search for competent speakers of the language who could teach it in a practical way, we met Joseph, who had retired prematurely from government service in Delhi and was available in the Kerala capital. Slim, with a gleaming brown dome, of indeterminate age, wearing a perpetually quizzical look and a general air of inscrutability, he had the appearance of an overgrown gnome. There was something about Joseph that immediately arrested the attention of those who met him. We hired him instantly, and he and I hit it off extremely well.

The academy, for various reasons, turned out to be short-lived, but the relationship with Joseph endured. I was struck by his intelligence, his dry wit, and his evident wisdom on subjects that ranged well beyond the mundane matter of expressing oneself effectively in English. When I was elected Member of Parliament for Thiruvananthapuram, I asked him whether he would join my staff.

For five years during my first term (2009–14), Joseph served loyally and effectively, handling routine correspondence and tackling unusual problems that were anything but routine. He regaled his colleagues in the office with his passing comments, often couched in a coruscating cynicism about the 'system' that not everyone easily understood. (He would later claim that he had deliberately kept one part of his brain from 'growing up', and it was from there that he generated his quirkiest thoughts.) On the side, he began peppering me with private emails, whose themes and treatment ranged from the sublime to the ridiculous, offering me his observations on politics, society, crime, music, religion, spirituality, sport—and Kerala in all its exhilarating and maddening ways.

When he moved on thereafter to the somewhat eccentric project of building himself a cottage in the hills where he and his wife could cultivate fruits and vegetables in the wild, we stayed in touch. His ideas and insights continued to come, sometimes erratically because of internet challenges in the uplands, but always insightful and stimulating.

I told Joseph that one day he should compile the decade and a half of advice he had given me into a book whose wit and wisdom would prove illuminating for generations yet to come. He resisted the temptation, or perhaps he was never tempted. Instead, last year, he offered me a manuscript that he had somewhat randomly put together, of aphorisms he had thought up. I was instantly captivated, and offered them to my publisher, David Davidar of Aleph, who years earlier had suggested that I write a book of aphorisms myself, for which I had never found the time.

David came back to say that, in his view, half of Joseph's scattershot thoughts were brilliant and the other half unpublishable. He returned to his original idea—would I be willing to collaborate with Joseph, retain the aphorisms he felt would work, and write the other half of the book? I immediately turned to Joseph—it was his project, after all, and he was fully entitled to withdraw his manuscript and submit it elsewhere, unchanged. But he leapt at the idea with delight, and gave me a free hand to revise, rework, and add to his original draft. I will always be grateful for his complete trust in me.

An aphorism is a concise statement or observation that expresses a general truth, principle, or nugget of wisdom, ideally in a memorable or witty manner. Aphorisms must be short, since they are intended to convey a profound or insightful idea with brevity, clarity, and wit. Sometimes aphorisms embody maxims, concise statements of a general principle or rule of conduct that serve as practical guidelines or advice for behaviour or decision-making. As a result, various philosophers expressed themselves in aphorisms, most famously the Roman Stoic philosopher Seneca the Younger (4 BCE–65 CE), who used aphorisms to explore themes of ethics, virtue, and human nature; the French writer and moralist François de La Rochefoucauld (1613–80), who titled his collection of aphorisms *Maxims* and delved into human behaviour, self-interest, and the complexities of social relationships; the German philosopher Friedrich Nietzsche (1844–1900), famed for asking 'Is man one of God's blunders? Or is God one of man's blunders?', who employed the aphoristic style extensively to interrogate morality, truth, and the nature of existence; and the Irish writer and playwright Oscar Wilde (1854–1900), whose literary works are filled with memorable and often humorous aphorisms about society, art, and human nature. Those are the gold standard, of course, but there have been numerous other individuals throughout history who have contributed to the development of aphoristic literature—most recently Nassim Nicholas Taleb, whose book of aphorisms, *The Bed of Procrustes*, published in 2010, included gems like 'True wealth is the ability to fully experience life,' and 'If you want people to read a book, tell them it is overrated.' So Joseph and I were walking gingerly on well-trodden ground. We sought to come up with insights from our own lived experience that were true for us and, as far as we were aware, had not been expressed by anyone else before—or, at least, not in quite the same way.

It took me several months to find the time for the reflection and thoughtful introspection that this process required, but earlier this year I came up with a manuscript I felt we could offer David. My own aphorisms included observations culled from years of writings and speeches, but also ideas I had mulled over but not actually put into words before. Together with Joseph's wholly original aphorisms, the pair of us have produced a volume we can both contentedly stand behind.

The inestimable David Davidar was, as usual, indispensable to the project, both by applying his rigorous editorial judgement on which aphorisms to delete or retain, and in editing some of them to the pithy cogency that marks the successful aphorism. It was he who changed Joseph's and my alphabetical format into a series of thematic chapters, reorganized the aphorisms appropriately, and commissioned the illustrations that adorn this book.

The excellent team at Aleph, led by Aienla Ozukum, has brought this book to press. I have always found Aienla an unobtrusive yet superbly competent editor to work with, and am grateful for her stewardship of the project. Bena Sareen has, as usual, done a splendid job on the cover, and this volume would not be what it is without Priya Kuriyan's elegant and whimsical illustrations.

Joseph and I are both in our mid-sixties; we have seen much of life, been moved and hardened by our experiences, and acquired some insights we believe it might be useful to pass on. We have no illusion that we have produced a masterpiece for the ages. But if something of the wisdom that has come our way pushes open a window in a reader's mind and lets some light in, this book will have served its purpose.

Shashi Tharoor
May 2023
New Delhi

1

THE MYSTERIES OF LIFE

1

Life is a paradox. We celebrate each birth even while knowing it comes with a sentence of death.

2

The easiest thing in life is letting go. It is also the hardest thing.

3

*Life is like passing through a room full
of clutter. And when we are finally
about to reach the door, the lights go off.*

4

*To live is to choose. Each day of living
is a day of multiple choices.*

5

*The less you expect from life,
the happier you are.*

6

Life is an interlude between a past of
non-existence and a future of non-existence.
We may as well enjoy whatever we can
of it while we exist.

7

Life is an oxymoron. It makes us want
an air-conditioned hell.

8

*There is, in short, no end to the story
of life. There are merely pauses. The
end is the arbitrary intervention of the
teller, but there can be no finality about
the choice. Today's end is, after all,
tomorrow's beginning.*

9

*Life teaches us only how to live.
We have to teach ourselves how to die.*

10

They advise us that we should not die before we actually die. But the problem is that dying is really a living thing.

11

The good thing about being a gravedigger is that you can always have the last laugh.

12

Life is actually a game of snakes and ladders played on a chessboard.

2

OF
HUMAN
NATURE

13

When people misjudge you or misunderstand you, they are revealing the limits of their own understanding.

14

The most dangerous hunters are those who prefer to hunt alone.

15

Some don't wear a mask, but they are
the only ones whose real face you won't
get to see.

16

Dislike, fear, and even hatred show you
care. Indifference is worse than all of these,
because it means you don't care at all.

17

Once you are sure about somebody it
would be a good idea to get a second
opinion about him from your dog.

18

Pharaoh Syndrome: the desire to carry our world along with us when we die.

19

The opposite of love is not hate.
It is pity.

20

Ugliness repels ugliness.
Same with beauty.

21

Sympathy is cheap.
Empathy hurts.

22

The more humility a man expresses in public, the greater his private opinion of himself.

23

Ask for sympathy,
and you will get loathing.

24

If you know the truth, don't reveal it.
Otherwise you will have to spend all
your time lying about it.

25

Trust a thief; never a reformed man.

26

Loyalty is only recognized when it is advertised. But the faithless are often the loudest in their affirmations of devotion.

27

Honesty is so rare that we often mistake it for cynicism.

28

Power is exercised; attraction is evoked.

29

If someone is silent, it doesn't mean that his or her brain is not working.

3

THE
SECRETS OF
SUCCESS AND
HAPPINESS

30

Happiness is found not by looking for it elsewhere, but by cultivating it within yourself.

31

Making the right decision too late is often worse than making the wrong decision early. You might still have time to correct your mistake.

32

Do and be damned.
Procrastinate and be double damned.

33

The fewer the choices available,
the easier decision-making is.

34

Achievers don't see frontiers;
they keep crossing them without noticing.

35

When you ask: know what you have to ask;
whom to ask; when to ask; and why you
have to ask.

36

The secret of happiness is to get your
mind to tell your brain to shut up and
mind its own business.

The single most important quality in any human being, whether a political leader, a cricket captain, or a spouse, is temperament. Charisma, intellect, and eloquence are no guarantee of success. A calm temperament can be trusted not to let you down.

List the things that irritate you about others. Then strike out all the items you can recognize in yourself.

39

Before you set out on a long journey,
settle with your banker, consult your
doctor, and warn your lawyer.
However, never inform your neighbour,
or your priest.

40

Aspire to set up institutions,
not to run them.

41

You are the only true judge of your own success. Only you know what it took and whether it has satiated the hunger inside you.

42

No amount of success will fulfil those who are never satisfied.

43

Fix an exorbitant price for something useless that you have, and then offer your best product for something slightly below that.

44

Learn exactly when to get into a debate, start a discussion, deliver a speech, make a sales pitch, and set an example. Once you do this you'll succeed in life.

45

The only good reason to be on this planet is to make a difference in the lives of others.

46

It is preferable to be alone than to waste one's time in mindless socializing.

47

Not all of us can do great things.
But we can all do ordinary things
as if they embody greatness.

48

Work in silence; let your success make all
the noise.

49

Be the best you that you can be.
No one can ever be a better you
than you yourself.

50

The most important question is not what
to do or how to live. It is why you live.
Once you know the answer to why,
the what and how will matter much less.

51

The best way to predict your future is to shape it yourself.

52

Kofi Annan, the late UN secretary-general, was a very wise man. This was one of his best-known aphorisms: 'Never hit a man on the head if you have your fingers between his teeth'.

53

The pessimist complains about the weather.
The optimist declares it will change.
The pragmatist goes out anyway,
with an umbrella.

4

THE ESSENCE
OF WISDOM

54

It is the fate of the wise to understand
the process of history and yet never to
shape it.

55

When the attitude is wrong, correction
is of no use. When the attitude is right,
there is no need for correction.

56

A philosopher is a lover of wisdom,
not of knowledge, which for all its great
uses ultimately suffers from the crippling
effect of ephemerality. All knowledge is
transient, linked to the world around
it and subject to change as the world
changes, whereas wisdom, true wisdom,
is eternal, immutable. To be philosophical,
one must love wisdom for its own sake,
accept its permanent validity and yet its
perpetual irrelevance.

57

Do the right thing and the outcome will
take care of itself.

58

When we argue with people smarter than
us we turn them into fools. Therefore,
avoid arguing with people who are
dumber than you.

59

An original opinion is rarer than a first edition. Most people's opinions are like second-hand books, well-thumbed by others.

60

Iron clothes inside out first, and see the difference! It's the same with self-improvement.

61

Judge another only after they have
walked a week in your shoes.

62

If you have to get kicked, it is better to
be kicked by an elephant than by an ass.

63

Knowledge is a harvest collected with pride, while wisdom is a gift accepted with humility.

64

When the fool points to the moon, the wise man does not look at the finger.

5

THE
NATURE OF
FOOLISHNESS

65

Keep a wary eye on the drunkard when he is sober.

66

The difference between ignorance and foolishness is that the fool is unaware of his own ignorance.

67

The foolproof plan rarely survives an encounter with a real fool.

68

The guru guides people to lead lives that he has no personal experience of living.

69

Know a little about almost everything,
and everything about almost nothing—
you will make a great conversationalist.

70

Clad in the guru's skin,
the ass spreads confusion far and wide.

71

We will be monkeys as long as we fail to
give up bananas.

72

*Fools search for the truth;
the wise let the truth find them.*

73

*The biggest problem with useless people
is that they make people around
them also useless.*

6

LEARNING
TO LEARN

74

In school you learn to answer the questions, in college to question the answers.

75

It is the questions that have to change, not the answers.

76

True education is what remains
in your head when you have forgotten
everything you learned for your examinations.

77

When you try to learn everything about
something you end up swallowing the
wrapper along with the chocolate.

78

The less you preach, the more you learn.

79

We have to wade into knowledge,
not jump into it.

80

If you are asked to choose between
learning more about the things you
already know, and the things you don't
know anything about, choose the former.

81

The best teacher is the one who prepares
his student to answer the questions the
teacher himself does not understand.

82

The good student is the one who tries
to find solutions even if he does
not fully understand.

83

The best student is the one
who tries to understand.

84

The worst student is the one
who only wants instruction.

85

Teaching is all about learning from those being taught.

86

The teacher's task is complete when the student becomes his equal and a friend.

Teaching and abuse are two things
which are most effective when halted
at the right moment.

A teacher needs to be evaluated only on
the basis of how useless his student has
turned out to be at the end.

There is no such thing as asking too many questions. That also means that there can never be too many answers.

7

BRAVERY AND COWARDICE

The only difference between courage and foolishness is that courage succeeds.

91

The courageous man acknowledges the world which is outside him and battles to the end. The coward gives up by proclaiming that the world is within himself and retreats within it.

92

The brave speak up for what they believe in. Cowards believe what they are told to speak up for.

93

The world is bearable to men who brush aside their state as helpless beings entrapped in an ordained web of fate, and courageously fight, asking why they have been wronged in an unfair and deranged conspiracy.

94

Better a gladiator who fights for reward,
than a slave who toils for wages.

95

*The thrill of the battle is more satisfying
than the spoils of victory.*

96

The seed cannot be what the tree is not.

8

SHADES OF
DESPAIR

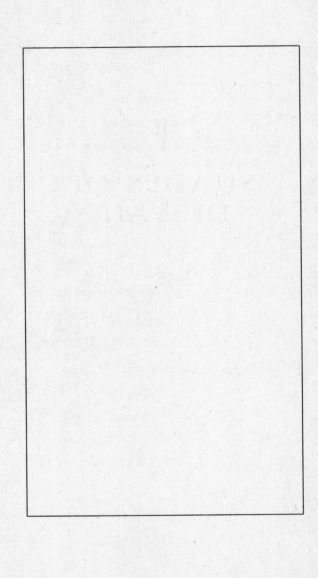

Grief and healing both come from within.
The most well-meaning friend cannot
reduce your grief or promote your healing.

98

The three most dangerous types
of men are:
(i) the defeated man;
(ii) the man with no vices; and
(iii) the man who is convinced that he
knows the truth.

99

The bond of shared suffering can be turned into the most potent force in the world.

100

Many a failure is the result of aiming too hard for success.

101

Every expression of sympathy masks relief
that it didn't happen to you.

Life is 100 per cent a failure because death is certain at the end of it.

9

ADVICE AND CRITICISM

103

The hardest challenge for most people is to follow the advice they give to others.

104

Good advice is that which stops in time.

105

Do not advise if you are later to judge.

106

Advice is the subtlest form of criticism.

107

The man who thinks he knows everything
needs to marry a woman
who actually does.

108

Criticism is free advice.
Gather as much as you can.

109

Flattery is usually listened to
more attentively than criticism.

110

When someone praises you, don't waste
your time standing there listening to it.
If someone criticizes you, take them out
for dinner so that you can hear more.

111

Adversity! Welcome it as a free check-up.

112

Kofi Annan, the legendary secretary-general of the United Nations, had a fund of aphorisms for every occasion. One of his favourites was the following: 'If the sharks bite you, do not bleed.' It took me years to understand what he meant. Never let your enemies have the satisfaction of seeing you suffer.

113

Kofi Annan again: 'Little boys only throw stones at trees that bear fruit'.

114

The most useful advice I have given others is to ignore my advice if it didn't accord with their gut sense of what was right for them.

10

FAMILY
AND OTHER
RELATIONSHIPS

115

Highly successful marriages require low expectations from at least one of the spouses.

116

Your glitter attracts the spouse you want. Its absence attracts the spouse you need.

117

Behind every successful man is a woman,
telling him he's not good enough.

118

The best partnership is when the partners
develop the confidence to not want the
other to treat them as anything but
themselves.

119

You are taught by your father,
but you learn from your mother.

120

The best thing we can do for the elderly
is to help them cut their toenails.

121

Early on in life I picked up the habit
of standing up each time someone I
respected passed by. That's the secret of
my fitness well into my old age.

122

Make your spouse your friend.
Sexual attraction fades; friendship endures.

11

FRIENDS
AND FOES

123

If you find yourself obliged to say something behind a person's back, make sure it is unsolicited praise.

124

Drop any friend who draws a line, because between real friends there can be no line.

125

Always seek the company of people who will speak in support of you when you are not there.

126

If you accept people as they are, you will eventually find something to like about them.

127

A friend is one who doesn't turn back
when you don't answer the doorbell.
He will climb in through the window to
check whether you are all right.

128

We cannot argue with our friends because
between friends there should be nothing
to argue about.

129

Spend your time with people for whom
how you are is more important than
who you are.

130

Sometimes it is better to lose an argument than to lose a friend.

131

Insincerity wins more friends and admirers than honesty does.

132

Only our enemies can show us up.
Thank God for enemies.

133

Overestimate your enemies,
underestimate your friends.

134

All my good friends left me one by one.
Now the only good friend left with me
is myself.

135

We have punished our enemies.
Now it is our turn.

The successful peacemaker knows that the fighters must be ready to want peace before turning to him to establish it.

12

THE WORKING
LIFE

The man who allows his job to define
him loses himself when the job ends.

138

He who spends his life climbing the
ladder will find he has no place to go
when the ladder falls.

139

Think twice before pulling up the ladder
when you climb out. You don't know
when you may fall in again.

140

The boss seeks 'freshers' with experience.
The leader attracts the experienced who
are still fresh.

141

Never drink with the boss.
Do not carry his bags either.

142

*Those who speak of the dignity of labour
are those whose own dignity comes from
avoiding all labour.*

143

The end of leisure is to avoid labour.

144

When you have people working under you
there is an easy way of getting promoted.
Harass your underlings in such a way
that they will work extra hard to get rid
of you by getting you kicked upstairs.

145

From 9 to 5, he earns his salary.
From 5 to 9, he earns his promotion.

13

THE RULERS
AND
THE RULED

146

Instruct superiors and you are only an adviser. Lord over inferiors and you are a petty dictator. But lead your equals and you'll be hailed a king.

147

The best king is not one who is feared or admired, but the one whose subjects believe all his achievements are their own.

148

Better to be a king who becomes a beggar
than a beggar who becomes a king.

149

The worst beggars are those who make
others beg for them.

150

The true leader does not hesitate to distribute credit and shoulder blame.

151

Pity the master who cannot exist without his slave.

A second-in-command can either be efficient or trustworthy. But not both.

153

Jesus rode into Bethlehem on an ass,
not an elephant. Justice and truth are
best delivered from the ground,
not from a throne.

14

OF GOD AND
THE DEVIL

154

The devil is a proud being.
He comes only when invited.

155

Think twice before telling someone to
go to hell. There's a good chance they'll
flourish there.

156

We humans are a peculiar species.
We pray loudly for the grace of God,
and quietly go in search
of the backing of the devil.

157

God keeps generating answers,
but we run around collecting them
only as questions.

158

If the devil arrives uninvited, continue
doing your work and tell him to either
wait, or go to hell.

159

We can either fear man and love God,
or love man and fear God. Never both.

160

Play! That's enough for the Creator who
has put us in this game.

161

Do not kill yourself. God is merciful.
He will kill you.

162

We are orphaned twice. First, when we
are born and God leaves us with our
parents. The second when our parents die
and return us to God.

163

The prayer that leads to understanding is more truthful than the understanding that leads to prayer.

164

It is safer to believe in God and be proved wrong, than to disbelieve and find out too late that you were wrong.

165

God is too dangerous to be let off as lazily as the agnostics and theists do.

166

Man seeks from God what he needs to obtain by himself.

167

The devil escorts you through heaven and
then dumps you in hell.
God takes you through hell and finally
leads you to heaven.

15

MATTERS OF
FAITH

168

There is only one heaven but many shades of hell. That is the problem, because the mind always runs after choices.

169

To speak of Hindu fundamentalism is a contradiction in terms, since Hinduism is a religion without fundamentals.

170

Every Hindu may not be conscious of the finer points of his faith, but he has been raised in the tradition of its assumptions and doctrines, even when these have not been explained to him. His Hinduism may be a Hinduism of habit rather than a Hinduism of learning, but it is a lived Hinduism for all that.

171

The problem with both the atheists and the theists is that both don't really know what God they are talking about.

172

The problem with any religion starts
when its priests discard the martyr's robes
for a shrink's coat.

173

Faith is sometimes a shield, often a
crutch. Beware of faith when it becomes
an ornament.

174

Fear no man, nor his god.

175

As Kofi Annan put it: 'The problem is never with the faith, but with the faithful'.

176

Man can create a god only in his own
image, reflecting all his strengths and
failings, and his desire for omnipotence
and dominance.

16

ETERNAL VERITIES

177

Man stands alone at the apex. All
other intelligent beings have successfully
thought themselves out of existence.

178

The hawk hunts, the crow picks,
the vulture waits.

179

Dissent is like a Gurkha's khukri. Once it emerges from its sheath it must draw blood before it can be put away again.

180

Let out anger through the back window, not the front door.

181

Every day has its dog.

182

*It is important to let sleeping dogs lie,
and to attack sleeping dogmas.*

183

*The moment you start explaining a truth
it starts degenerating into falsehood.*

184

Only the truth, and nothing other than
the truth, shall set you free.

185

Search not for honest men, for you won't
find any. Instead search for men who at
least had honest fathers.

186

Don't cage horses, or untie asses.

187

A robot's biggest strength is that it has no feelings. That is also its biggest weakness.

188

There are two types of restaurants; those
which have fat waiters and
thin managers, and those which have
thin waiters and fat managers.
Choose wisely between the two.

189

Beware the young philosopher,
and the old saint.

190

The best stories are the ones told to oneself.

191

*No tale is more important than the way
the tale is told.*

192

Words can hurt, but not as much as silence.
Words may be lashes; silence is poison.

193

Words are all we have. But words matter
because of the thoughts they embody, and
their capacity to change minds.

194

If you can express your love in words,
you have already diminished it.

195

The only art that matters is art that
elicits a response—that provokes emotion,
reflection, passion, anger, action or
reaction, it doesn't matter, as long as it
does not elicit indifference.

196

The glass is neither half-full nor
half-empty. It is a glass—and it is waiting
for you to pour something into it.

17

GLIMPSES OF HISTORY

197

The British are the only people in history crass enough to have made revolutionaries out of Americans.

198

One of the lessons history teaches us is that history often teaches us the wrong lessons.

199

Every Indian must forever carry with him,
in his head and heart,
his own history of India.

200

Ours is a country where both history and
truth can be modified by a possessive
pronoun. There is my history and your
history, his truth and her truth.

201

The British had the gall to call
Robert Clive 'Clive of India' as if he
belonged to the country, when all he
really did was to ensure that much of the
country belonged to him.

202

Some foolishly seek to revenge themselves upon history. They do not understand that history is its own revenge.

203

Socrates spoke; Plato wrote; Aristotle acted.

204

Use the sword of Damocles to cut the
Gordian knot.

18

FACETS OF
INDIA

205

India has been born and reborn scores of
times, and it will be reborn again.
India is forever, and India is forever
being made.

206

The only possible idea of India is that of
a nation greater than the sum of its parts.

207

*India is not, as people keep calling it,
an underdeveloped country, but rather,
in the context of its history and cultural
heritage, a highly developed one in an
advanced state of decay.*

208

*One strength of the Indian mind is
that it knows some problems cannot be
resolved and it learns to make the best of
them. That is the Indian answer to the
insuperable difficulty. One does not fight
against that by which one is certain to
be overwhelmed; but one finds the best
way, for oneself, to live with it. This is
our national aesthetic. Without it, India,
as we know it, could not survive.*

209

India is a thali, a collection of
sumptuous dishes on a common platter.
Each dish is in a separate bowl and does
not necessarily mix with the next, but
they belong together and combine on your
palate to give you a satisfying repast.

Indians do well in any situation that calls for an instinctive awareness of the subjectivity of truth, the relativity of judgement, and the impossibility of action.

211

Does NRI (Non-Resident Indian) stand for Not Really Indian or Never Relinquished India? I believe a little of both! Today the NRIs are the National Reserve of India.

212

Bureaucracy is simultaneously the most crippling of Indian diseases and the highest of Indian art forms.

213

We Indians are notoriously good at being resigned to our lot. Our fatalism goes beyond, even if it springs from, the Hindu acceptance of the world as it is ordained to be.

214

Pluralist India must, by definition, tolerate plural expressions of its many identities.

215

India imposes no procrustean exactions on its citizens: you can be many things and one thing.

In India we celebrate the commonality of major differences; we are a land of belonging rather than of blood.

217

We all have multiple identities in India;
we are all minorities in India.
Our heterogeneity is definitional.

218

Our founding fathers wrote a
Constitution for their dreams. We have
given passports to their ideals.

Democracy is not just elections every five years, but what happens between them.

The instinctive Indian sense is that nothing begins and nothing ends. We are all living in an eternal present in which what was and what will be is contained in what is, or to put it in a more contemporary idiom, that life is a series of sequels to history.

221

Indian nationalism is the nationalism of an idea, the idea of an ever-ever land, emerging from an ancient civilization, shaped by a shared history, sustained by pluralist democracy.

222

Question: Who wrote the Constitution of India?
Answer: It is there in the first five words of the Preamble:
'We the People of India....'

A NOTE ON THE BOOK

The aphorisms numbered 1, 2, 4, 5, 6, 8, 13, 16, 21, 22, 26, 27, 28, 30, 31, 33, 37, 41, 42, 45, 46, 47, 48, 49, 50, 51, 53, 54, 56, 57, 59, 66, 67, 68, 69, 74, 76, 78, 81, 82, 83, 84, 89, 90, 92, 97, 100, 101, 103, 104, 106, 107, 109, 114, 115, 116, 117, 122, 123, 125, 126, 129, 130, 131, 136, 137, 138, 142, 145, 147, 150, 164, 166, 169, 170, 179, 182, 187, 191, 192, 193, 194, 195, 196, 197, 198, 199, 200, 201, 202, 205, 206, 207, 208, 209, 210, 211, 212, 213, 214, 215, 216, 217, 218, 219, 220, and 221 have been written by Shashi Tharoor and copyright in these aphorisms vests in Shashi Tharoor.

The aphorisms numbered 3, 7, 9, 10, 11, 12, 14, 17, 18, 19, 20, 23, 24, 25, 29, 32, 35, 39, 40, 43, 58, 60, 63, 64, 65, 70, 72, 73, 75, 77, 79, 80, 85, 86, 88, 93, 94, 95, 96, 102, 108, 110, 111, 118, 119, 120, 121, 124, 127, 128, 132, 133, 135, 139, 140, 141, 143, 148, 149, 151, 152, 154, 155, 156,

157, 158, 159, 160, 161, 163, 165, 167, 168, 171, 172, 174, 176, 177, 180, 181, 183, 184, 185, 186, 188, 190, 203, 204, and 222 have been written by Joseph Zacharias and copyright in these aphorisms vests in Joseph Zacharias.

The aphorisms numbered 15, 34, 36, 38, 44, 55, 61, 62, 71, 87, 91, 98, 99, 105, 134, 144, 146, 153, 162, 173, 178, and 189 have been jointly written by Shashi Tharoor and Joseph Zacharias, and copyright in these aphorisms vests in Shashi Tharoor and Joseph Zacharias.

The aphorisms by Kofi Annan numbered 52, 112, 113, and 175 have been recorded by Shashi Tharoor.

INDEX

The index is organized by page numbers.